Where Animals Live

Freshwater Animals

By Katie Buck

 I see snails in fresh water.

I see turtles in fresh water.

I see mussels in fresh water.

I see newts in fresh water.

 I see otters in fresh water.

I see eels in fresh water.

I see frogs in fresh water.

I see prawns in fresh water.

I see crayfish in fresh water.

I see beavers in fresh water.

I see fish in fresh water.

I see water striders
in fresh water.

Word List

vocabulary words

freshwater	mussels	prawns
fresh	newts	crayfish
water	otters	beavers
snails	eels	fish
turtles	frogs	striders

73 Words

I see snails in fresh water.

I see turtles in fresh water.

I see mussels in fresh water.

I see newts in fresh water.

I see otters in fresh water.

I see eels in fresh water.

I see frogs in fresh water.

I see prawns in fresh water.

I see crayfish in fresh water.

I see beavers in fresh water.

I see fish in fresh water.

I see water striders in fresh water.

CHERRY BLOSSOM PRESS

Published in the United States of America by Cherry Lake Publishing Group
Ann Arbor, Michigan
www.cherrylakepublishing.com

Photo Credits: © ShayneKayePhoto/Shutterstock, cover; © WildlifeWorld/Shutterstock, title page; © Fauzan Maududdin/Shutterstock, 2; © KARI K/Shutterstock, 3; © KRIACHKO OLEKSII/Shutterstock, 4; © Rudmer Zwerver/Shutterstock, 5; © DejaVuDesigns/Shutterstock, 6; © COULANGES/Shutterstock, 7; © Wayne Wolfersberger/Shutterstock, 8; © Arunee Rodloy/Shutterstock, 9; © Vaclav Matous/Shutterstock, 10; © P Harstela/Shutterstock, 11; © Ryno Botha/Shutterstock, 12; © Jan Miko/Shutterstock, 13; © Hintau Aliaksei/Shutterstock, 14

Note from publisher: Websites change regularly, and their future contents are outside of our control. Supervise children when conducting any recommended online searches for extended learning opportunities.

Cherry Blossom Press is an imprint of Cherry Lake Publishing Group.

Library of Congress Cataloging-in-Publication Data

Names: Buckley, Katie (Children's author), author.
Title: Freshwater animals / written by Katie Buckley.
Description: Ann Arbor, Michigan : Cherry Blossom Press, [2024] | Series: Where animals live | Audience: Grades K-1 | Summary: "Freshwater Animals showcases animals found in a freshwater environment, including animals like otters and eels. Uses the Whole Language approach to literacy, combining sight words and repetition. Simple text makes reading these books easy and fun. Bold, colorful photographs that align directly with the text help readers with comprehension"— Provided by publisher.
Identifiers: LCCN 2023035086 | ISBN 9781668937587 (paperback) | ISBN 9781668939963 (ebook) | ISBN 9781668941317 (pdf)
Subjects: LCSH: Freshwater animals—Juvenile literature. | Freshwater ecology—Juvenile literature.
Classification: LCC QL141 .B83 2024 | DDC 591.76—dc23/eng/20230906
LC record available at https://lccn.loc.gov/2023035086

Printed in the United States of America

Katie Buckley grew up in Michigan and continues to call the Mitten her home. When she's not writing and editing, you'll find her gardening, playing music, and spending time with her dog, Scout. She has always loved books and animals, so she's a big fan of this series.